Knitting with beads is a special branch of the love of needlework. The stunning array of beads available today allows you to make dozens of exquisite pieces of jewelry and wonderful wearables that just sparkle!

Most projects knitted with beads are very portable. The beads are pre-strung, so there are no loose beads to put on after knitting has begun.

And since only the hands and wrists move, knitting with beads is ideal for travel and office waiting rooms. This makes handwork easy for busy people to complete valued projects.

With a wide array of beads and projects to choose from, you are sure to find several in this book that inspire you to start right away.

Mary Libby Neiman

Reversible Bracelet
page 12

Crystal Bracelets
page 13

Patchwork Bracelet
pages 14-15

Rope Necklace
page 11

Opal & Crystal Necklace
pages 16-17

Focal Bead Necklace
pages 18-19

Drop Earrings
pages 24-25

Twist & Turn Bracelets
pages 26-27

Purple Bead Necklace
pages 28-29

Tasseled Lariat
pages 30-31

Lariat with Slide
pages 32-33

Strawberry Pin
pages 40-41

Small Bag
pages 42-43

Pink Poncho
pages 44-45

Lightning Hat
pages 46-47

Knitted Cuffs
pages 48-49

Beaded Tassels
pages 50-51

New Metallics #1 Gold

New Metallics #22 Pink Tourmaline

New Metallics 2 Ply

YLI Jean Stitch

Gudebrod #F weight Silk Twist

Coats & Clark Opera

Anchor/Coats & Clark #8 Pearl Cotton

Merino wool DK weight

Knitting with Beads
Basic Information

In most knitting with beads, every row is knit and knit with a bead or beads in each stitch. As it is knit, the beads are on the back of the work. Since beads are usually knit in every row, beads will eventually appear on both sides. When every row is a knit row, that is called Garter stitch.

Knitting that incorporates occasional beads in a pattern is often referred to as beaded knitting. In beaded knitting, the bead is placed into the Knit stitch and will be seen on the front of the knitting, as it is knit. This makes it easier to catch a mistake because you will not have to turn your work over to check the back side. The basic pattern in most knitting with beads is alternate rows of Knitting and Purling.

Knitting with beads is most appropriate for the intermediate to skilled knitter. Good knitting requires an understanding of knitting terms and abbreviations, the ability to read a pattern, skill in holding the needle and thread as stitches are made, as well as achieving proper tensioning. It is better to practice these skills without the added complications of stringing, manipulating and positioning beads in the knitted work.

Many projects, especially those featuring small glass beads, specify very small needles and slim thread. It takes practice to work comfortably with these tools and supplies.

Choosing Thread or Yarn

Choose thread or yarn for bead knit jewelry that is firm and not stretchy.

A knitted structure is naturally stretchy and that means many bracelets knitted with beads will not need a clasp. Knitted items also have a memory, so a bracelet will expand or stretch to slide over a hand and then contract to fit nicely at the wrist. If a bracelet looks too big after it stretches to slide over your hand, simply squeeze it into a smaller shape around your wrist by encircling the bracelet with your thumb and forefinger and pressing evenly. While knitting does have a memory, when thread is covered with beads it sometimes needs help to recall its original size.

A stretchy yarn may eventually lose some of its stretch and leave an item with a sloppy fit. Non-stretchy yarn provides a firm bed for the beads to nest in and the beads will sit evenly in their rows. Non-stretchy yarn allows for firm and even tensioning when knit.

Choosing Beads

Choose beads for knitted garments carefully. Because garments need washing, do not choose dyed beads or beads with delicate surface finishes that may be affected by even gentle washing soaps. When using glass beads in knitted projects, special care should be taken when washing. One helpful trick is to line the sink or container used for washing with a piece of old terry towel or a doubled piece of sheeting. This will keep glass beads from ever hitting the porcelain or metal of the container.

Do not use glass beads on garments for infants or small children. Small fingers and small mouths will often be attracted to shiny objects. Even small plastic beads can sometimes break or be pulled off of knitting.

Choose wood, plastic, or metal beads rather than glass for any active wear garment such as ski hats.

6° Japanese seed beads

4mm cube beads

6mm faceted crystal

8° hex beads

6° Czech Republic seed beads

4mm faceted crystal

Swarovski 4mm Crystal bicones

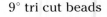

8° seed beads

9° tri cut beads

11° seed beads

Glass "chips"

Dagger beads

Needles for Knitting with Beads

Two different types of needles are used for knitting with beads: knitting needles and beading needles.

Knitting Needles

Most of these projects for knitting with beads, specify the use of 0000 double pointed (dp) steel knitting needles. These have traditionally been sold in packages of five and are often used in knitting socks with very fine yarns. Traditionally, they are 8" long. 4" 0000 dp steel needles are now available and some retailers will also sell pairs of the needles.

These steel needles are very smooth and sharp. Putting an earring back or a pin clutch on the non-working end of each needle will prevent some accidental poking in the arm or torso. These ends are temporary and can be removed.

One advantage of using these removable ends is that, when stopping your knitting before the project is finished, the end can be removed from the empty needle and placed on the point of the needle with stitches. The needle with an earring back on both ends is now a stitch holder. This is especially nice because the weight of the beads combined with the smooth thread and the shiny steel needles create a situation where stitches of the partially knitted item can easily slide off the needle. Because the stitches are fairly small, they are difficult to transfer to a standard stitch holder.

Gluing a wood, plastic or glass bead permanently to one end of each needle is preferred by some knitters. These permanent ends will not accidentally come off. An earring back occasionally may disconnect itself from the fine steel needle.

For projects knitted with beads, choose any standard knitting needle of the correct diameter and length. Plastic, aluminum and wood/bamboo needles are the most popular. Most new needles are also marked with the mm size as well as U.S. or other size. Most new patterns will also specify mm size. This conforms to the new standards established by the Craft Yarn Council to move toward worldwide uniform markings on knitting needles.

Beading Needles

The choice of a beading needle is largely determined by two factors, the size of the hole in the beads to be used and the size of the knitting yarn. Ideally, the yarn will thread easily through the eye of the beading needle and the bead hole will be large enough to pass easily over the entire beading needle.

Big Eye beading needles will accommodate a wide range of yarns and beads. Essentially the "hole" runs most of the length of the needle and they are quite easy to thread. They are also the most expensive needle to buy.

Twisted wire needles come in several sizes. The most popular for Beaded Knitting stringing are 12 and 16. The large eye is easy to thread and compresses to a smaller profile when the first bead is pulled over the needle and onto the thread or yarn.

Sewers often prefer their familiar sharps or milliners needles. Beaders often prefer their familiar #11 or #12 beading needles. #22, #24 and #26 tapestry needles work well for many finishing tasks and offer the advantage of a blunt point. Be sure to test the needle chosen for stringing with the thread and the beads to be used.

Helpful Accessories

A few useful tools include small sharp scissors, a bead scoop and a really good glue such as Hypo Cement. Hypo Cement, with its long narrow dispenser tip, is ideal for applying small amounts of glue precisely to a small area. When dry, it is clear and not brittle.

Beading Needles

10" 0000 steel Rosewood 3.75 mm

Size 11 Knitting Needles

L-R: #22 & 24 Tapestry Needles, #16 Steel Twisted wire

John James Needles #12

Bead Scoop

Glue

Why Do I Need to Make a Bobbin?

Bead Knitting includes beads in the stitches. Beads are strung onto the thread before any stitches are made and add weight to the thread. It is important to manage this weight so it does not pull too much on the thread or your hand as you work. One way to control this weight is to wind the beaded thread onto a bobbin. Winding a bobbin prevents a tangled mess of beads and wasted thread.

You may want to make more than 1 bobbin. It is difficult to manage more than 2 yards of beads at one time. It is easier to string and knit 2 yards of beads, stop, cut the working thread, tie the next bobbin thread to your working thread, and continue.

Or add beads to the other end of the thread.

Make a Bobbin

Wind thread and beads on a stiff cardboard bobbin to store your 'inventory'.

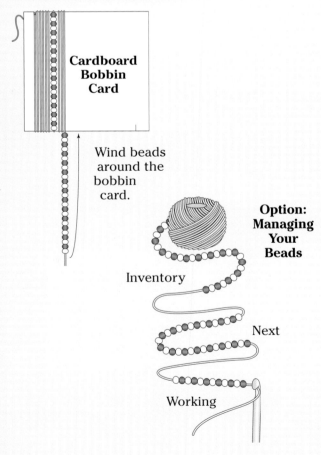

Cardboard Bobbin Card

Wind beads around the bobbin card.

Inventory

Option: Managing Your Beads

Next

Working

Knitting with 0000 dp Knitting Needles

For novice knitters, knitting with beads on 0000 double pointed knitting needles will require some practice. Since a firm, non-stretchy yarn or thread is required to keep beads in neat order after knitting, for most projects, you will be knitting with your yarn only on the last inch or two of the needle. In other words, you will be knitting off the tips because the yarn will not stretch to travel any distance to the tip.

At first this will seem daunting, but practice with a strong plain thread like *Coats and Clark* Opera or *DMC* Cebelia and 6° seed beads will help accustom your hands and eyes to working with the 0000 needles. Whether you knit English style or Continental, with practice and a positive attitude, you will be able to master knitting on 0000 knitting needles. The bonus is that once you have become comfortable knitting with these needles, you will find their light weight and small size make knitting less tiring.

Let There Be Lights

Good natural light is the best tool you can have for knitting with beads. A lamp with a natural daylight bulb will also give you the illumination you need. This light and proper corrective glasses, if you need them, will enable you to see details better and there will be less strain on your eyes.

Stringing Bead Patterns

If you are stringing a pattern, check and double-check your bead sequence before beginning to knit. It is so much easier to correct a mistake now. If you make a sample of a few inches of your pattern (at least one repeat) and tape that to your work table, you can check for accuracy every few minutes, as you string the beads you need for your project. A color photocopy of your bead sequence will also work nicely for checking.

Enough Is Enough?

Always buy a bit more thread and beads than the pattern calls for. The amounts in these patterns are estimates of what will actually be needed. You may have a larger wrist or neck or prefer a more relaxed fit. Differences in tension will change the amount of thread used. Some types of beads have colors that may vary from lot to lot.

Knot Finished

When knitting with beads and fine thread, it is wise to secure thread ends with a pair of "beaders' knots". Thread a wire or small tapestry needle with the cut end of your thread, and bring the needle to the reverse side, leaving a small loop on the top side. Bring the needle back to the top side, passing it through the loop, before pulling on the thread to tighten. Repeat once more and place a small amount of Hypo Cement on the thread at the point where it exits the loop. Let dry, then cut. When larger needles and yarn are used to knit with beads, usually the ends are not glued, but carefully woven back into the knitting at a seam or edge.

Small Gauge

Large Gauge

Size and Gauge

Patterns for knitting with beads do not always refer to gauge, the number of stitches knit per inch and the number of rows needed to produce 1" of knitting. Because beads of the same specification, for example, 8° seed beads, will vary in size depending on the country of origin and even with manufacturers in the same country, bead knit patterns will often specify the length that should be knit. The length knit can be adjusted to allow for a good fit.

Most knitting with beads should be done very firmly. Keep good tension on the thread as it is knit and tighten the tension a bit more at the end of each row before turning to begin the next row.

Knitting with beads usually means the beads cover the knitting stitches. Because mostly beads and very little thread is seen, an area where tension has varied is easily seen because the beads will not be as tight and regular in their rows. Uneven tension when knitting with glass beads will be enhanced by the reflective quality of the glass. Check tension often. Because knitting with beads brings beads to the back of the work, look at the back of rows with more than two or three beads before tightening your tension on the last stitch of a row. If tension has become slack in the beginning or middle of a row, tightening the thread at the end will not help early stitches.

Making a practice swatch with the actual beads and thread to be used in a pattern is helpful. If there are enough beads and thread available, keep these swatches instead of undoing them, and sew them onto squares of mat or foam board. Add the name of the thread, the bead size and the needles used. Keep these together to refer to when planning a new project.

More About Gauge

Knitting with beads usually does not change the gauge of standard knitting without beads. If occasional beads are added to a knitted fabric, no size adjustments need to be made to a pattern. The tension should not change in areas where beads are knit or it will distort the knit fabric.

It is recommended that a gauge swatch be made before knitting any garment. If there are beads in the pattern for the garment, then include some beads in the swatch. Mounting and identifying the yarns, beads and needles used will soon build a nice library of swatches to refer to in planning new projects.

Knitting
Basic Steps and Stitches

Refer to a book on knitting for detailed instructions on how to knit.

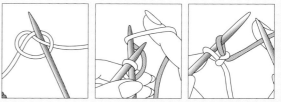

1. Begin with a row of foundation stitches worked each stitch onto one needle. Make a slip knot, leave a 4" tail, pull the stitch taut.

2. Add foundation stitches by using a second needle and your finger to loop thread into stitches.

3. Keep foundation stitches on one needle. Add as many as needed.

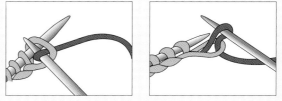

KNIT: Add each knit stitch with loops to the <u>front</u> thru the foundation stitches.

Slip each knit loop from the left needle to the right needle.

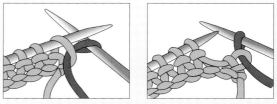

PURL: Add each purl stitch with loops to the <u>back</u>.

Slip each purl loop to the right needle.

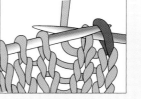

BIND OFF: End by binding off on the last row.

On the last row, stitches are secured 'off the needle'.

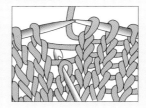

Correct a 'dropped stitch' with a crochet hook. Pull a loop from each row until you have a row of stitches.

Beginner

Narrow Spiral Bracelets

Soft and flexible, these narrow bracelets will dress up jeans or add a bit of flash to your favorite silk blouse in the evening.

SIZE: 8"

MATERIALS:
10 yards very strong thread
8° seed beads
   (150 color of A and 150 of
   color B or 300 of one color)
1 pair 0000 dp knitting needles
Twisted wire needle
#24 tapestry needle
Hypo Cement

STRING THE BEADS:
2 color A seed beads, then 2 color B seed beads on 5 yards of doubled thread. Continue string-ing pattern until all 300 beads are strung.

INSTRUCTIONS:
Cast on 3 stitches leaving a 10" tail with the needle attached.
Row 1: Knit 3 stitches.
Row 2: Slip 1 stitch purl-wise, slide 1 bead, Knit 1 stitch • slide 1 bead, Knit 1 stitch.
Rows 3 – 151:
Repeat Row 2.
Cast off leaving 8" tails.

Knitting Spirals

    This bracelet must be knit very firmly. For optimum spiral effect, at the end of each row, adjust your tension by tugging on the thread, tightening the two stitches you have just knit. • Check the fit of the bracelet before finishing. Use a large safe-ty pin to temporarily join the ends of the bracelet. Make sure the two ends are touching with no gaps. Narrow your hand and slide or roll the bracelet over your hand and onto your wrist. If the bracelet seems too large, adjust the size by removing as many rows as needed to get a better fit. Be sure to retest any size to be certain it will slide on over your hand. Remember that knitting has "give" so it will stretch a bit to slide or roll on. Knitting will also "rebound" to its original size after stretching.

    Connect the two ends of the bracelet by Needle Weaving the two ends together, using a figure 8 pattern. Place one thread through the eye of a #24 Tapestry and insert the needle behind the last bead knit. Bring the thread under that bead and then up through the space between the two ends and over the first bead on the other end. Then insert the needle down into the space between that bead and the first bead in the next row. Continuing sewing in this figure 8 pattern two more times.

    Check to see that there is no gap between the two ends and that the beads in the first row knit and the last row knit are almost touching. If there is a gap or excess stitches showing, continue stitching until join is firm and tight.

    Finish with knots and glue. Repeat finish by knotting and gluing any remaining thread.

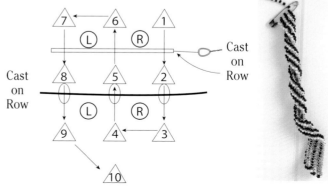

Big Spiral Knit Bracelets

by Mary Libby Neiman

Bracelets knitted with beads have a silky smooth feel that makes them a joy to wear.

These are particularly easy to string because you only have one color. Whether you love rich malachite or iridescent purple, you are going to enjoy wearing these pretty accessories.

SIZE: 8"

MATERIALS:
18 yards very strong thread
425 of one color 6° seed beads
1 pair 0000 dp knitting needles
Twisted wire needle
#24 tapestry needle
Hypo Cement

STRING THE BEADS:
425 seed beads on 9 yards of doubled thread. Distribute beads along 9 yards of thread as the thread is rewound onto a bobbin, leaving 1 yard bare to begin knitting.

INSTRUCTIONS:
Cast on 6 stitches leaving a 9" tail with the needle attached.
Row 1: Knit 6 stitches.
Row 2: Slip one stitch purl-wise • *slide 1 bead, Knit 1 stitch • repeat from * 4 times for a total of 5 bead knit stitches.
Row 3: Slip one stitch purl-wise, knit 5 stitches.
Rows 4 –170:
Repeat Rows 2 and 3.
  Cast off leaving 8" tails. Do not cast off too tightly or your ends may not match well.

Knitting Spirals

As you knit, you will notice that the knitting spirals. The side of the knitting with the beads showing will be on the outside of the spiral.

If you have a very small hand, you may need to stop knitting at Row 130 (65 rows of beads). For a medium hand, less than 170 rows will work. Stop and check for fit as you knit.

This bracelet must be knit very firmly. For optimum spiral effect, at the end of each row, adjust your tension by tugging on the thread, tightening the stitches you have just knit.

Check the fit of the bracelet before finishing

Connect the two ends of the bracelet by Needle Weaving the two ends together, using a figure 8 pattern. Place one thread through the eye of a #24 Tapestry and insert the needle behind the last bead knit. Bring the thread under that bead and then up through the space between the two ends and over the first bead on the other end. Then insert the needle down into the space between that bead and the first bead in the next row. Continuing sewing in this figure 8 pattern 5 more times.

Check to see that there is no gap between the two ends and that the beads in the first row knit and the last row knit are almost touching. If there is a gap or excess stitches show, continue stitching until join is firm and tight. Finish with knots and glue. Repeat finish by knotting and gluing any remaining thread.

Lariat Necklace

by Mary Libby Neiman

Once strictly reserved for royalty, purple and gold twist together in a lariat fit for a queen.

SIZE: 46"

TIP:
When knitting with beads on one side only you will use approximately 4" of doubled thread to every 1" of beads. Whenever you wind thread and beads onto a working bobbin, keep this in mind. Wind 1 complete wrap of beads, then 3 complete wraps of thread only. Beads will be contained and controlled on the bobbin and not put extra weight on the working thread. They will unwind for use in knitting just when you need them. You will always need about an extra 24" of thread to hold for tensioning.

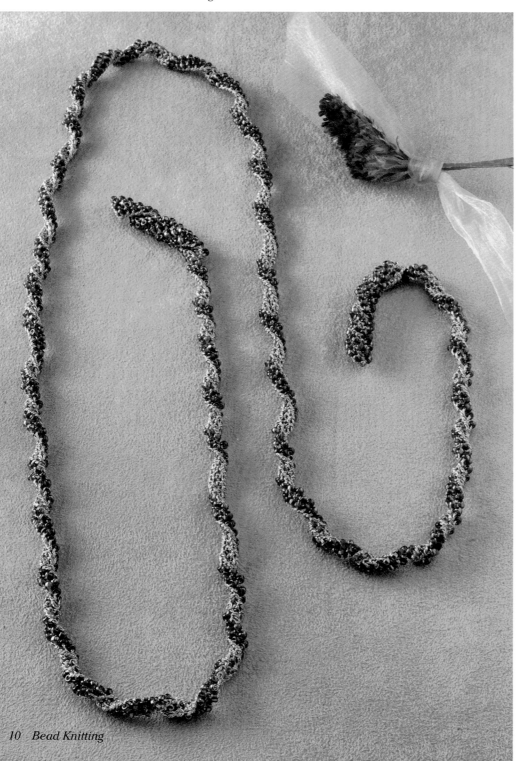

MATERIALS:
50-60 yards Gold Metallic thread
1100 (approximately 1 ounce or 28 grams) Plum AB 8° seed beads
1 pair 0000 dp steel knitting needles
Hypo Cement

STRING THE BEADS:
String all of the beads on 30 yards of doubled thread. You may find it easier to string one third to one half of the beads and knit those beads before adding more. To get to the thread end you must add the rest of the beads to, wind the finished knitting around a 4" x 4" matboard bobbin. Then continue winding most of the remaining thread around the bobbin. Add the beads. Hook the end of the thread into the notch of the original bobbin and wind all but 1 yard of the thread and all but 5" of the strung beads back onto the original bobbin.

INSTRUCTIONS:
Cast on 5 stitches.
Row 1: Knit 5 stitches.
Row 2: Slip 1 stitch purlwise • *slide a bead • Knit • Repeat from * for a total of 4 bead Knit stitches.
Row 3: Slip 1 stitch purlwise • Knit 4 stitches.
Rows 4-40: Repeat Rows 2 & 3
Row 41: Slip 1 stitch purlwise • Knit 2 stitches together • Knit 2 stitches together.
There should be 3 stitches remaining.
Row 42: Slip 1 stitch purlwise • *slide a bead • Knit • repeat from * for a total of 2 bead Knit stitches
Row 43: Slip 1 stitch purlwise • Knit 2 stitches.
Rows 44-450 (approximately 42"): Repeat Rows 42 & 43.
Row 451: Slip 1 stitch purlwise • *increase 1 stitch in the next stitch • repeat from * 1 time. Five stitches should be on the needle.
Row 452: Slip 1 stitch purlwise • *slide a bead • Knit • repeat from * for a total of 4 bead stitches.
Row 453: Slip 1 stitch purlwise • Knit 4 stitches.
Row 454-492: Repeat Rows 452 & 453.

Cast off.
Bury, knot, glue and trim your tails.

As you knit, you will notice that the knitting spirals. The four bead rows spiral even more. Hold the Lariat in the center, letting the two halves hang down and adjust any twists so that they are even and going in the same direction.

Rope Necklace
by Mary Libby Neiman

Knit a romantic rasp-berry and gold rope neck-lace that will match all your new spring outfits and go with your winter holi-day wardrobe too!

This color combination is too versatile to pass up and so irresistible you will want to make this one first.

SIZE: 43"

TIP:
When knitting with beads on one side only you will use approximately 4" of doubled thread to every 1" of beads. Whenever you wind thread and beads onto a working bobbin, keep this in mind. Wind 1 complete wrap of beads, then 3 complete wraps of thread only. Beads will be contained and controlled on the bobbin and not put extra weight on the working thread. They will unwind for use in knitting just when you need them. You will always need about an extra 24" of thread to hold for tensioning.

MATERIALS:
46-52 yards Gold Metallic thread
1000 (approximately 1 ounce or 28 grams) Gold Luster Raspberry 8° seed beads
1 pair of 0000 dp steel knitting needles
Hypo Cement

STRING THE BEADS:
String all of the beads on 26 yards of doubled thread. You may find it easier to string one third to one half of the beads and knit those beads before adding more. To get to the thread end you must add the rest of the beads to, wind the finished knitting around a 4" x 4" matboard bobbin. Then continue winding most of the remaining thread around the bobbin. Add the beads. Hook the end of the thread into the notch of the original bobbin and wind all but 1 yard of the thread and all but 5" of the strung beads back onto the original bobbin.

INSTRUCTIONS:
Cast on 3 stitches.
Row 1: Knit 3 stitches.
Row 2: Slip 1 stitch purlwise • *slide a bead • Knit • repeat from * for a total of 2 bead Knit stitches.
Row 3: Slip 1 stitch purlwise • Knit 4 stitches.
Rows 4-420 (approximately 41 inches): Repeat Rows 2 & 3.

Cast off.

As you knit, you will notice that the knitting spirals. Hold the necklace in the center, letting the two halves hang down and adjust any twists so that they are even and going in the same direction. Match a bead row to a bead row and needle weave the two ends together. Bury, knot, glue and trim your thread tails.

Beginner

On the Surface

Slender 2-ply metallic thread with polyester core.

Red and Purple

SIZE: 8"

MATERIALS:
16-18 yards of strong metallic thread (Red or Purple F weight silk thread would also work)
8° Delica beads
  (360 Red, 360 Purple Metallic)
Gold charms (1 purse, 1 handbag, 2 shoes)
4 Gold jump rings
1" long Gold multi strand clasp
1 pair 0000 dp knitting needles
Twisted wire needle
Hypo Cement

STRING THE BEADS:
String 6 Red beads then 6 Purple beads onto 9 yards of doubled thread. Repeat until all the beads are strung.

INSTRUCTIONS:
Cast on 7 stitches leaving 10" tails.
Row 1: Knit 7 stitches.
Row 2: Slip 1 stitch purlwise (needle in front) but keep the thread to the back of the needle holding the stitches. *Slide 1 Purple bead, Knit 1 stitch. Repeat from * 5 more times for a total of 6 stitches knit with beads.
Row 3: Slip 1 stitch purlwise (needle in front) but keep the thread to the back of the needle holding the stitches. *Slide 1 Red bead, Knit 1 stitch. Repeat from * 5 more times for a total of 6 stitches Knit with beads.
Rows 4-121: Repeat Rows 2 & 3.

Cast off very carefully, taking care not to pull on the thread too much. The width of your cast on row and of your cast off row should be the same. Cut thread leaving 10" tails.

Using the tail threads, sew one end of the knit bracelet to one row of loops on the clasp. Repeat with the other end. Bury, knot, glue and trim all the tails.

Attach two charms to one end loop on the clasp with a Gold jump ring. Repeat with the other two charms to the other end loop.

Easy

Charming Reversible Bracelet

by Mary Libby Neiman

This charming bracelet was designed to be fun to wear.

The charms are attached to the end loops of the multi strand clasp so they can always be seen whether the Red or the Purple side is showing.

Teal and Copper

photo facing page 13

You can make a reversible bracelet in any colors you want. Check out this stunning combo in copper and teal. Like black, copper goes with almost anything, and it always adds a touch of elegance.

SIZE: 8"
Follow the instructions for Charming Red and Purple Reversible Bracelet. Just change the bead colors.

Crystal, Red, and Purple Flat Band Bracelet

Red and purple really sparkle when paired with crystal in this reversible bracelet. Make one to wear to your next outing with your Red Hat Ladies group.

SIZE: 8"

MATERIALS:
16-18 yards of strong Silver Metallic thread
8° hex beads (540 Silver Lined Crystal, 180 Purple, 180 Red)
1 pair 0000 dp knitting needles
Twisted wire needle
Hypo Cement

STRING THE BEADS:
String 1 Crystal, 1 Purple, 1 Crystal, 1 Purple, 2 Crystals, 1 Red, 1 Crystal, 1 Red, 1 Crystal onto 9 yards of doubled thread. Repeat until all the beads are strung. Stop every 3 or 4 rows and check your pattern.

Crystal	Purple	Crystal	Purple	Crystal
Crystal	Red	Crystal	Red	Crystal

INSTRUCTIONS:
Cast on 7 stitches leaving 10" tails.
Row 1: Knit 7 stitches.
Row 2: Slip 1 stitch purlwise (needle in front) but keep the thread to the back of the needle holding the stitches. *Slide 1 Purple bead, Knit 1 stitch. Repeat from * 5 more times for a total of 6 stitches Knit with beads.
Row 3: Slip 1 stitch purlwise (needle in front) but keep the thread to the back of the needle holding the stitches. *Slide 1 Red bead, Knit 1 stitch. Repeat from * 5 more times for a total of 6 stitches Knit with beads.
Rows 4-121: Repeat Rows 2 & 3.

Cast off very carefully, taking care not to pull on the thread too much. The width of your cast on row and of your cast off row should be the same. Cut thread leaving 10 inch tails. Needle weave the bracelet ends together. Knit and glue all threads.

These beautiful and easy bracelets make great gifts.

Patchwork Pattern Bracelet

by Mary Libby Neiman

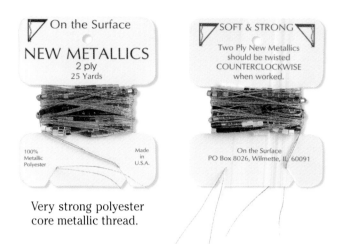

Very strong polyester core metallic thread.

Wear bright colors that go with anything to work, and then turn your bracelet over for an evening of classic black, white, copper, gold, and silver to match any item in your wardrobe.

The patchwork bracelet is reversible. It is more difficult to load the beads for a two-sided bracelet. Careful attention must be paid to the pattern and it is important to check the beads after each color sequence to be certain the correct number of beads have been threaded. This bracelet can also be very attractive with a pattern on one side only and a coordinating color on the other side.

SIZE: 8½"

MATERIALS:
30-34 yards New Metallic thread (Silk buttonhole twist also works well)
Approximately 6 grams each of 16 colors of 8° Japanese hex beads
1 pair 0000 dp steel knitting needles
#14 or 16 twisted wire needle
Tapestry needle (#22 or #24)
4" x 4" matboard bobbin
Hypo Cement

STRING THE BEADS:
String beads as follows: Measure 15-17 yards of doubled thread and wind all but 2 yards onto a bobbin. Insert doubled thread through the eye of the needle. One half of the beads could be strung now and balance after the first half of the bracelet is knit, but when "back loading" the balance of the beads, the pattern must be strung in reverse.

4 color A, 4 color B, 4 color C, 4 color D
Repeat for a total of 5 times.

4 color E, 4 color F, 4 color G, 4 color H
Repeat for a total of 5 times.

4 color I, 4 color J, 4 color K, 4 color L
Repeat for a total of 5 times.

4 color M, 4 color N, 4 color O, 4 color P
Repeat for a total of 5 times.

INSTRUCTIONS:
Cast on 9 stitches.
Row 1: Knit 9 stitches.
Row 2: Slip 1 stitch purlwise (needle in front) but keep the thread to the back of the needle holding the stitches. *Slide 1 bead, Knit 1 stitch. Repeat from * 7 times for a total of 8 stitches Knit with beads.

Row 3 and every row after Row 3 until all the beads are knit and the bracelet measures the correct length: Repeat Row 2.
Cast off.

Check length and fit of the bracelet. Pin cast on and cast off ends together carefully and make sure the bracelet will fit over your hand. An assistant to help with this size check is helpful.
Cut thread at cast off end leaving a 10" to 12" tail.
Joining: Sew the two ends of the bracelet together by needle weaving the ends of the cast off threads from one end of bracelet to the other end. Needle weaving can also be done with a single thread and repeated with the other thread. Do not sew the cast on row to the cast off row or you will not get a good join. These two rows are especially stretchy and if they are stitched into to join, a lot of extra thread will show in the join.

The first stitch of the join should be made into the knitted area behind the first row of knitting on the cast off edge. The thread should then be brought under the first bead and then over the first bead on the other (cast on) edge and into the knitted area just behind that bead.

Repeat this figure 8 stitching, moving along one bead per stitch until 9 stitches have been made on each edge. Check your stitches as you work, turning the bracelet "inside out" as you stitch to check both sides.

Stitch all loose ends, one at a time, into the bracelet. Knot and glue each end. Trim ends.

TIP: With a strong foam board or matboard bobbin to support the weight of the beads, it is possible to string all the beads at once.

Once the beads have been properly loaded and checked, the pattern work is done. The beads will automatically make the pattern since every stitch, except the first stitch in every row, is knit with 1 bead.

Occasionally, even after careful checking, a mistake in the color sequence will occur. If one bead is missing, simply knit that stitch without a bead and sew the missing bead in place later. If there is one more bead than there should be of a color, carefully, break that bead. Before breaking a bead, insert the tip of a needle into the bead and pull the knitting thread behind the needle so that it will be protected from any sharp edges when the bead is broken. The other option is to break the threads, repair the pattern by adding or removing beads and overlap the old thread and the new thread while knitting them together for 2 or 3 stitches. If the threading error is on the edge of the pattern, break the thread a few stitches before the error so your join will be in the center of the knitting row.

This pattern is knit with 8° Japanese hex beads. 8° Czech hex beads also come in some very nice colors but they tend to be smaller than the Japanese beads. If Czech beads are used, the bracelet pattern may have to be adjusted to get the correct length.

Add a touch of magic with the beautiful edge on this charming bracelet.

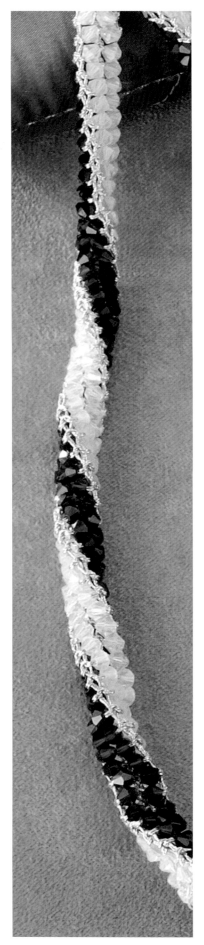

Easy

Opal and Swarovski Crystal Necklace

by Mary Libby Neiman

Genuine crystal beads combine with a handmade perforated clasp to make a special fancy necklace. The clasp is so beautiful, you can wear it in front.

The pattern for this gorgeous necklace is simple. Two crystal beads are knit on each side and the necklace spirals around and around as it is knit.

SIZE: 21" including clasp

MATERIALS:
24 yards strong metallic thread
4mm bicone Crystal beads (290 White Opal, 298 Cobalt)
HandFast Hand wrought Sterling Silver clasp
1 pair 0000 dp knitting needles
Twisted wire needle
Hypo Cement

STRING THE BEADS:
String 2 Opal, 2 Cobalt. Repeat until only 8 Cobalt beads remain. Reserve 8 Cobalt beads to embellish perforated clasp.

INSTRUCTIONS:
Cast on 3 stitches.
Row 1: Knit 3 stitches.
Row 2: Slip 1 stitch purlwise • *slide a bead • Knit 1 stitch • repeat from * for a total of 2 bead Knit stitches.
Rows 3-292 : Repeat Row 2.

Cast off leaving a 14" tail. Use cast on thread tails to sew one end of the necklace to the toggle part of the clasp. Use one cast off thread tail to sew the other necklace end to the main piece of the clasp. Use the other thread tail to stitch the 8 reserved cobalt beads to the top of the clasp. Knot, glue and trim thread tails.

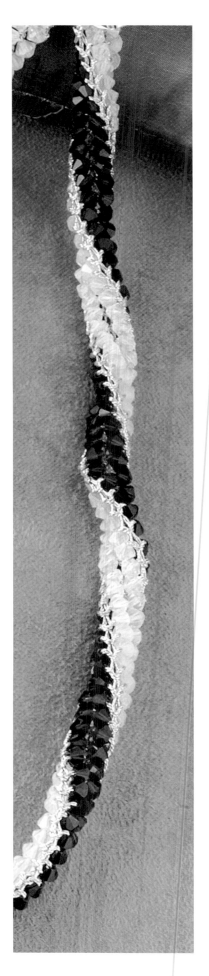

**Make this
sparkling crystal
necklace
to dress up
every ensemble.**

Easy

Bead Knit Necklace with Focal Bead
by Mary Libby Neiman

Knitting with beads provides a very attractive canvas for showing off the focal bead on this necklace.

The challenge with focal beads is to complement the color and design of the bead without drawing attention from the beautiful bead.

SIZE: 21" including clasp

MATERIALS:
30 yards *YLI* Jeans Stitch thread
8° seed beads (80 color A, 80 color B, 80 color C, 80 color D)
1 *Tom Boylan* Focal bead
1 Gold toggle clasp
1 pair 0000 dp knitting needles
Twisted wire needle
Hypo Cement

STRING THE BEADS:
Section 1 Stringing:
Measure 7 yards of doubled thread.
String *2 color A, 2 color B, repeat from * 4 times for a total of 5 pairs of each color.
*2 color C, 2 color A, repeat from * 4 times for a total of 5 pairs of each color.
*2 color D, 2 color C, repeat from * 4 times for a total of 5 pairs of each color.
*2 color B, 2 color D, repeat from * 4 times for a total of 5 pairs of each color.
Repeat the stringing pattern 3 times for a total of 4 repeats.

Section 2 Stringing:
Repeat stringing directions for Section #1.

INSTRUCTIONS:
Two identical 9" pieces are to be knit.
Section 1 Knitting:
Cast on 3 stitches leaving a 10" tail.

YLI Jeans Stitch polyester thread is strong and easy to knit with.

Row 1: Knit 3 stitches.
Row 2: Slip 1 stitch purlwise • *slide a bead • Knit 1 stitch • repeat from * for a total of 2 bead Knit stitches.
Rows 3-91: Repeat Row 2.
Cast off leaving a 12" tail.
Section 2 Knitting:
Repeat Section 1 knitting instructions.

Joining :
Join the two sections through the focal bead. Be sure your join is very tight and secure. Tails from Section 1 are first stitched behind the last bead knit in Section 1. The thread passes through the focal bead and is stitched behind the last bead knit in Section 2. Each of the 4 tails should pass through the focal bead 2 times. Bury, knot, glue, and trim the thread tails.

The other end of each section is then stitched to the clasp pieces. Section 1 can be stitched to the toggle bar and Section 2 is then stitched to the circle. Bury, knot, glue, and trim the thread tails.

**Show off
a fabulous focal
bead on this
stunning necklace.**

Open Spiral Bracelet

by Mary Libby Neiman

This open spiral bracelet is knit with the same bead colors as the open spiral necklace. The finished look is more delicate but still dramatic.

SIZE: 9"

MATERIALS:
12 yards strong smooth Black polyester, silk or metallic thread
279 Gold Iris 8° seed beads
279 Black 11° seed beads
1 pair 0000 dp knitting needles
Twisted wire needle
Hypo Cement

STRING THE BEADS:
Measure: 6 yards of doubled thread and wind all but 2 yards onto a bobbin.
Insert doubled thread through the eye of the needle.
String 3 Gold Iris 8° seed beads • String 3 Black 11° seed beads • repeat until all beads are strung.

INSTRUCTIONS:
It is important to knit this with firm even tension to keep the spiral as open and crisp as possible. Keep every stitch tight and remember to tighten again at the end of each row.
Cast on 4 stitches leaving 8" tails.
Row 1: Knit 4 stitches.
Row 2: Slip 1 stitch purlwise • *slide a Gold Iris 8° bead • Knit 1 stitch • repeat from * for a total of 3 bead Knit stitches.
Row 3: Slip 1 stitch purlwise • *slide a Black 11° bead • Knit 1 stitch • repeat from * for a total of 3 bead Knit stitches.
Rows 4 – 93: Repeat Rows 2 & 3.
Cast off leaving 8" tails.
Stitch the two ends together firmly and evenly. Bury, knot glue and trim tails.

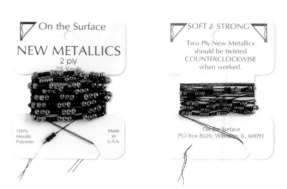

Slim and strong metallic polyester thread allows beads to move easily into position for knitting.

Open Spiral Necklace

Classic and dressy... this dramatic necklace and bracelet show off one of the fancy beads, Gold Iris. To highlight this special color, the thread and the "other side" beads are both Black. As with all bead knitted spirals, extra twists can be manipulated before clasping to shorten the necklace.

SIZE: 21" including clasp

MATERIALS:
34 yards strong smooth Black polyester, silk or
    metallic thread
516 Gold Iris 6° seed beads
516 Black 8° seed beads
Gold toggle clasp
1 pair 0000 dp knitting needles
Twisted wire needle
Hypo Cement

STRING THE BEADS:
Measure: 17 yards of doubled thread and wind all but 2 yards onto a bobbin. Insert doubled thread through the eye of the needle.
String 3 Gold Iris 6° seed beads • String 3 Black 8° seed beads • repeat until all beads are strung.

INSTRUCTIONS:
It is important to knit this with firm even tension to keep the spiral as open and crisp as possible. Keep every stitch tight and remember to tighten again at the end of each row.
Cast on 4 stitches leaving 10" tails.
Row 1: Knit 4 stitches.
Row 2: Slip 1 stitch purlwise • *slide a Gold Iris 6° bead • Knit 1 stitch • repeat from * for a total of 3 bead Knit stitches.
Row 3: Slip 1 stitch purlwise • *slide a Black 8° bead • Knit 1 stitch • repeat from * for a total of 3 bead Knit stitches.
Rows 4 – 343: Repeat Rows 2 & 3.
Cast off leaving 10" tails.
    Attach one end of the necklace to one side of the clasp. Attach the other end of the necklace to the other piece of the clasp.

Easy

Fiesta Spiral Bracelets

by Mary Libby Neiman

These bracelets are fascinating because the spiral appears to have no beginning or end. They get their depth and texture from two different sizes of beads.

SIZE: 9"

MATERIALS for each bracelet:
12 yards strong smooth Black polyester, silk or metallic thread
279 large 6° seed beads (Red, Turquoise, or Yellow)
279 small 8° seed beads (Yellow or Blue)
1 pair 0000 dp knitting needles
Twisted wire needle
Hypo Cement

STRING THE BEADS:
Measure: 6 yards of doubled thread and wind all but 2 yards onto a bobbin. Insert doubled thread through the eye of the needle.
String 2 large 8° seed beads • 2 small 11° seed beads • repeat until all beads are strung.

INSTRUCTIONS:
It is important to knit this with firm even tension to keep the spiral as open and crisp as possible. Keep every stitch tight and remember to tighten again at the end of each row.
Cast on 4 stitches leaving 8" tails.
Row 1: Knit 4 stitches.
Row 2: Slip 1 stitch purlwise • *slide a large 8° bead • Knit 1 stitch • repeat from * for a total of 3 bead knit stitches.
Row 3: Slip 1 stitch purlwise • *slide a small 11° bead • Knit 1 stitch • repeat from * for a total of 3 bead knit stitches.
Rows 4 – 93: Repeat Rows 2 & 3.
Cast off leaving 8" tails. Stitch the two ends together firmly and evenly. Bury, knot, glue and trim tails.

It's fun to collect these Easy-to-make Spiral Bracelets.

Pink Teardrop Earrings

These delightful earrings are light and sparkling. The Pink is knit with all one color bead and matching thread. Graduated size beads knit into a teardrop shape. A different look is achieved by knitting with Red beads and contrasting Gold thread. The Red earrings are four rows shorter than the Pink earrings and use four fewer beads.

by Mary Libby Neiman

SIZE: 1" not including ear wires

MATERIALS:
3 yards of strong metallic, silk or polyester thread
8 Crystal 5mm faceted round beads
16 Crystal 5mm bicone beads
10 Crystal 4mm bicone beads
1 pair of lever back earrings
1 pair 0000 dp knitting needles
Hypo Cement

STRING THE BEADS:
String on doubled thread Five 4mm bicone beads • Eight 5mm bicone beads • Four 5mm round faceted beads

INSTRUCTIONS:
Cast on 3 stitches leaving 7" tails.
Row 1: Knit 3 stitches.
Row 2: Slip 1 stitch purlwise • slide one 5mm round bead, Knit 1 stitch • slide one 5mm round bead, Knit 1 stitch.
Row 3: Knit 3 stitches.
Rows 4 & 5: Repeat Rows 1 & 2.
Row 6: Slip 1 stitch purlwise • slide one 5mm bicone bead, Knit 1 stitch • slide one 5mm bicone bead, Knit 1 stitch.
Row 7: Knit 3 stitches.
Rows 8-13: Repeat Rows 6 & 7.
Row 14: Slip 1 stitch purlwise • slide one 4mm bicone bead, Knit 1 stitch • slide one bead 4mm bicone, Knit 1 stitch.
Row 15: Knit 3 stitches.
Row 16 & 17: Repeat Rows 6 & 7.
Row 18: Knit 2 stitches, slide one 4mm bicone bead, Knit 1 stitch.
Row 19: Knit 2 stitches together, Knit that stitch together with the last remaining stitch. One stitch remains. Cut a 10" tail and bring tail through the last stitch and tighten.
Use 10" tails to sew knitted beads to lever back earring. Bury, knot, glue and trim thread.
Stitch 7" tails into the knitting. Knot, glue and trim.
Repeat stringing and construction for the other Pink earring.

SIZE: 1½" not including ear wires

MATERIALS:
3 yards of Silk metallic or polyester thread
56 Crystal 4mm bicone beads
1 pair of lever back earrings
1 pair 0000 dp knitting needles
Hypo Cement

STRING THE BEADS:
String 28 beads on doubled thread for each earring.

INSTRUCTIONS:
Cast on 3 stitches leaving 7 inch tails.

Row 1: Slip 1 stitch purlwise • slide one bead, Knit 1 stitch • slide one bead, Knit 1 stitch.

Row 2: Knit 3 stitches.

Rows 3-14: Repeat Rows 1 & 2.

Row 15: Knit 2 stitches together, Knit that stitch together with the last remaining stitch. One stitch remains. Cut a 10" tail and bring tail through the last stitch and tighten.

Use 10" tails to sew knitted beads to lever back earring. Bury, knot, glue and trim thread. Stitch 7" tails into the knitting, knot, glue and trim. Repeat stringing and construction for the other earring.

Crystal Drop Earrings

by Mary Libby Neiman

Three yards of thread and fifty-six bicone beads combine to make an enticing pair of Crystal earrings. Experiment with contrasting thread for an added touch of elegance. For example, use gold thread with the blue opal beads and silver thread with the aurora borealis beads. The tighter this is knit, the firmer the earring. Even if they are firm, they will still swing sweetly from the metal earring. If they are knit too loosely, they will not spiral as well and more of the thread will be visible.

Crystal earrings knitted with beads have a great advantage over other similar styles because they are incredibly light, making them oh-so-comfortable to wear.

Pair of Twist and Turn Bracelets

by Mary Libby Neiman

On the Surface

NEW METALLICS
2 ply
25 Yards

Slender 2 ply metallic thread with polyester core allows beads to move easily into position for knitting.

These bracelets can be worn side by side as a pair. They can also be twined around each other to create a big bangle. The two can also be connected end to end to make a necklace. The bead knitted bead project on page 29 shows how to make a bead that can slide on the two "end to end" bracelets to cover one of the clasps.

The zig-zag pattern is created when beads of dramatically different sizes are knit in alternating rows. Tightly tensioning the thread as each bead is knit also helps give a firm shape to the bracelet.

STRING THE BEADS:
On 5 yards of doubled thread, string two 4mm cube beads, then two 8° seed beads. Continue stringing pattern until all 160 beads of each size are strung.

INSTRUCTIONS:
Cast on 3 stitches leaving a 10" tail with the needle attached.
Row 1: Knit 3 stitches.
Row 2: Slip 1 stitch purlwise, slide 1 cube bead, Knit 1 stitch • slide 1 cube bead, Knit 1 stitch.
Row 3: Slip 1 stitch purlwise, slide one 8° seed bead, Knit 1 stitch • slide one 8° seed bead, Knit 1 stitch.
Rows 4-161: Repeat Rows 2 & 3.
Cast off leaving 8" tails.

This bracelet must be knit very firmly For optimum Zig-Zag spiral effect, at the end of each row, adjust your tension by tugging on the thread, tightening the two stitches you have just knit. Sew one side of the bracelet to one side of the clasp. Sew the other side of the bracelet to the other side of the clasp. Repeat the directions to knit a matching bracelet.

'Twist and Turn' Pair of Bracelets

To twist the bracelets into the large round shape, hold up the same clasp end of each bracelet with the thumb and finger of one hand while the rest of each bracelet hangs down freely, side by side. Use your free hand to gently twist them together.

You will notice that they tend to "nest" as they twist. This is a good thing and will help you guide the pair of bracelets into a single round bracelet. Connect the clasps.

Only the cube beads will be visible when the bracelets are twisted together.

SIZE: 9½"

MATERIALS for each bracelet:

10 yards of very strong thread

160 of any color of 4mm cube beads

160 of any color of 8° seed beads

1 "snap clasp"

1 pair of 0000 dp knitting needles

Twisted wire needle

Hypo Cement

Create a pair
of versatile
'Twist and Turn.
bracelets.

Easy

Purple Bead Knitted Bead
by Mary Libby Neiman

Making a knitted bead is a glorious way to turn two bracelets into a necklace with a knitted embellishment. Knitted beads also make interesting embellishments for necklaces or single bracelets.

Knitting a swatch to help determine a good fit is recommended. In a shaped bead like this one you will only need to knit all 19 rows of the bead with the three smallest beads to see if you have the correct number of rows to be large enough to slide onto the bracelet/necklace.

SIZE: 2" long, 3½" around

MATERIALS:
13 yards strong polyester, metallic or silk thread
9 Purple Iris 6mm faceted beads
9 Purple Iris 4mm faceted beads
36 Matte Purple Iris 4mm cube beads
36 Matte Purple Iris 6° seed beads
36 Purple Metallic 6° seed beads
36 Matte Purple Iris 8° seed beads
72 Burgundy Metallic 8° seed beads
1 pair 0000 dp knitting needles
Twisted wire needle
Hypo Cement

STRING THE BEADS:
String on 6½ yards of doubled thread: 1 Matte Purple Iris 8° bead • 2 Burgundy Metallic 8° beads •1 Purple Metallic 6° bead •1 Matte Purple Iris 6° bead •1 Matte Purple Iris 4mm cube bead • 1 Purple Iris 4mm faceted bead •1 Matte Purple Iris 4mm cube bead • 1 Matte Purple Iris 6° bead • 1 Purple Metallic 6° bead • 2 Burgundy Metallic 8° beads • 2 Matte Purple Iris 8° bead •2 Burgundy Metallic 8° beads •1 Purple Metallic 6° bead • 1 Matte Purple Iris 6° bead •1 Matte Purple Iris 4mm cube bead • 1 Purple Iris 6mm faceted bead • 1 Matte Purple Iris 4mm cube bead •1 Matte Purple Iris 6° bead • 1 Purple Metallic 6° bead • 2 Burgundy Metallic 8° beads • 1 Matte Purple Iris 8° bead.

INSTRUCTIONS:
Cast on 14 stitches leaving 7" tails.
Row 1: Knit 14 stitches.
Row 2: Slip 1 stitch purlwise *slide 1 bead, Knit 1 stitch • repeat from * 12 more times for a total of 13 bead Knit stitches.
Row 3: Knit 14 stitches.
Rows 4 – 19: Repeat Rows 2 & 3.
Cast off and cut thread leaving 15" tails.

With one of the 15" tails, seam the cast off and cast on rows together, firmly and carefully. Check often to see that there are no gaps or uneven areas.

TIP: Baste the seams together carefully with a contrasting color. Place a pencil through the hole in the basted bead while finished stitching is completed with the tail threads. Remove basting thread.

Bury, knot, glue and trim tails.

**Add a
knitted bead
as the center
of interest to a
beautiful necklace.**

Intermediate

Lariat with Tasseled End

by Mary Libby Neiman

Lariats make a truly versatile addition to a jewelry wardrobe. A long lariat can even be worn as a belt. The knitted body of this lariat is 54", each end terminating with a handmade bead and 2" tassel. A lariat is easily tied with a simple knot or it can be wrapped once more, doubling the special effect. This length can even circle the neck a third time for a real jewelry triple play.

Lariats can be anchored in even more varied wrappings with the addition of a special bead knitted bead. This bead becomes even more useful if it remains open…without being sewn shut. Sewing magnetic clasps inside the four corners allow the bead to appear closed when it encircles two or more elements of the lariat body. See how many different ways you can wear this.

SIZE: 58"

MATERIALS:

For the knitted body:
58 yards strong metallic thread
1000 (approximately 1 oz) Matte Rose AB 8° seed beads
1000 (approximately 1 oz) Rose AB 8° seed beads
2 coordinating handmade beads
1 pair 0000 dp knitting needles
Twisted wire needle
Hypo Cement
For the tassels:
1½ yards beading thread
30" Rose 9° AB tri cut beads
9 Green 3mm faceted crystal beads
10 Champagne 3mm faceted crystal beads
9 Champagne 4mm faceted crystal beads
19 Dark Rose 4mm faceted crystal beads

10 Dark Rose 3mm faceted crystal beads
10 Light Green dagger beads
#10 beading needle

STRING THE BEADS:
String for section 1: 364 Matte Rose AB 8° seed beads.
String for section 2: 3 Matte Rose AB 8° seed beads, 1 Rose AB 8° seed bead • repeat 90 times.
String for section 3: 2 Matte Rose AB 8° seed beads, 2 Rose AB 8° seed beads • repeat 90 times.
String for section 4: 1 Matte Rose AB 8° seed bead, 3 Rose AB 8° seed beads • repeat 90 times.
String for section 5: 364 Rose AB 8° seed beads.

The body of the lariat will take approximately. 29 yards of doubled thread. You may choose to string Section 1 and knit it. Then add the beads for Section 2, knit Section 2, then 3, 4, & 5.

INSTRUCTIONS:
Section 1:
Cast on 3 stitches leaving a 14" tail.
Row 1: Knit 3 stitches.
Row 2: Slip 1 stitch purlwise • slide 1 bead, Knit 1 stitch • slide 1 bead, Knit 1 stitch.
Rows 3-182: Repeat Row 2.
Stop now and add beads for Section 2.
Rows 182-364: Repeat Row 2
Stop now and add beads for Section 3.
Rows 365-547: Repeat Row 2
Stop now and add beads for Section 4.
Rows 548-739: Repeat Row 2.
Stop now and add beads for Section 5.
Rows 739-921: Repeat Row 2.
Cast off, cut thread leaving 14" tails.

Tasseled Ends:
Pass 1 pair of thread tails through the eye of a twisted wire needle. Bring this thread through 1 large handmade bead.
Remove 1 tail from the needle and string *12 tri cut 9° beads, 1 Green 3mm bead, 8 tri cut 9°, 1 Champagne 4mm, 4 tri cut 9°, 1 Dark Rose 4mm, 1 tri cut 9°.
Bring threaded needle back through the Dark Rose 4mm bead, then up through the rest of the strung beads that follow including the large bead. Pass the needle through the end of the lariat, then through one side of the lariat and back down through the large bead.
Repeat with the other thread tail. Now two "legs" of the tassel are complete.
Usually the hole in the large bead is too small to allow 18 passes of the knitting thread. To complete the remaining 7 "legs" of the tassel thread a # 10 beading needle with a 14" length of strong fine beading thread. Bring the needle up through the large bead, leave 7" hanging down from the bead hole. Pass the needle through the lariat, side to side and then back down through the large bead. Follow the stringing sequence from * finishing with knotting and gluing after passing back up through the sequence and into the body of the lariat. Repeat threading and stringing and knotting with the other fine 7" beading thread.
Repeat with two more pieces of 14" beading thread to make 9 "legs". Knot off the remaining long thread.
Tassel #2.
Pass thread tail from the other end of the lariat through the other large handmade bead.
Then follow directions for the tassel #1 with two changes.
String 12 tri cut 9° beads, 1 Champagne 3mm bead, 8 tri cut 9° beads, 1 Dark Rose 4mm, 4 tri cut 9°, 1 Dark Rose 3mm, 1 Green dagger, then back up through all the beads before knotting and gluing. The 2nd change is that 10 beaded tassel "legs" are strung.

Lariat with Rose Bead Slide

by Mary Libby Neiman

Create a stunning focal bead for your lariat necklace by knitting a simple rectangle and attaching magnetic clasps. When you close the clasps, you have a gorgeous bead slide that complements your necklace perfectly.

SIZE: 1½" x 2" when opened flat

MATERIALS:
12 yards strong polyester metallic or silk thread
30 Raspberry 8° seed beads
30 Pink Opal 8° seed beads
30 Raspberry 8° hex beads
30 Raspberry 6° seed beads
30 Silver Lined Rose 6° seed beads
15 Gold Luster Rose 4mm cube beads
2 pair small flat magnetic clasps
1 pair 0000 dp knitting needles
Hypo Cement

STRING THE BEADS:
String on 5 yards of doubled thread: 1 Raspberry 8° seed • 1 Pink Opal 8° • 1 Raspberry 8° hex • 1 Raspberry 6° seed • 1 Silver lined Rose 6° • 1 Gold Luster Rose 4mm cube • 1 Silver lined Rose 6° • 1 Raspberry 6° seed • 1 Raspberry 8° hex • 1 Pink Opal 8° •1 Raspberry 8° seed • repeat this sequence for a total of 17 groups.

INSTRUCTIONS:
Cast on 12 stitches leaving 8" tails.
Row 1: Knit 12 stitches.
Row 2: Slip 1 stitch purlwise • *slide 1 bead, Knit 1 stitch repeat from * until all 11 beads are knit.
Row 3: Slip 1 stitch purlwise • Knit 11 stitches.
Rows 4-18: Repeat Rows 2 & 3
Cast off carefully. Be certain that stitches are not pulled too tightly. This cast off row must be the same length as the cast on row. Cut leaving 10" tails.

Sew 1 part of each magnetic clasp inside the very corner of the cast off row. Check to be sure that you sew the other half of each clasp in the corner on the same side. When the second half of each clasp is positioned for sewing, it should be placed ¼" in from the corner (**see photo for placement**). Sew these clasps in place very tightly. They will be closed and pulled apart many times so the strong knitting thread tails should be used and the knotting and gluing of the tails are even more important. Test and double-test, joining and pulling the magnetic clasps apart to be sure they are secure.

Create a stunning focal bead for your necklace.

Knit Beads
by Mary Libby Neiman

A variety of bead knitted beads combine to make a bold bright necklace. The three smallest beads are simply knitted strips of beads joined into a circle. There is no support inside these beads. The other 9 beads are sewn together around wood beads. The wood beads help keep the bead shape. Bali Silver spacer beads complete this exciting look.

SIZE: 15" beaded portion of necklace

MATERIALS:
80 yards Turquoise 2 ply metallic thread
For each small bead: 18 Teal/Green 6° seed beads
For each medium bead: 45 assorted including 8° seed bead, 6° seed beads, and 4 mm cube beads
For each large bead: 77 assorted 8°, 6°, 4 mm cube and 6 mm faceted beads
For the center bead: 108 assorted 8°, 6°, 4 mm cube and 6 mm faceted beads
16 Bali Silver spacer beads
Small Silver crimp clasp
20" slim cord
1 pair 0000 dp knitting needles
#24 Tapestry needle
Twisted wire needle
Needle-nose pliers
Hypo Cement

STRING THE BEADS:
For each small bead: 18 Teal/Green 6° beads.
For each medium bead: One 8°, One 6°, One cube, One 6°, One 8°, repeat 8 times.
For each large bead: One 8°, One 6°, One cube, One faceted, One cube, One 6°, One 8°, repeat 10 times.
For the center bead: One 8°, Two 6°, One cube, One faceted, One cube, Two 6°, One 8°, repeat 11 times.

INSTRUCTIONS:
For each bead, cast on 1 more stitch than the number of beads in each stringing sequence.
Row 1: Knit every cast on stitch.
Row 2: Slip 1 stitch purlwise, slide 1 bead, Knit 1 stitch, repeat until all the beads in the sequence are knit.
Row 3: Knit every stitch.
Rows 4-12: (for small beads) repeat Rows 2 & 3.
Rows 4-19: (for medium beads) repeat Rows 2 & 3.
Rows 4-23: (for large beads) repeat Rows 2 & 3.
Rows4-25: (for center bead) repeat Rows 2 & 3.
      Cast off, making sure thread is not pulled too tightly. Cut thread leaving a 12" tail.
For small beads, seam ends together.
For medium beads, seam together around an oval bead.
For large beads, seam ends together around an oval bead.
For center bead, seam ends together around an oval bead.
Finish: Alternately string spacer beads and knitted beads on slim cord as in photo. Attach clasp to the ends.

Create a bold
bright necklace
with simple
knitted beads.

Sl st = Slipstitch

Bk st = bead knit stitch

Intermediate

Wavy Edge Bracelet

by Mary Libby Neiman

This bracelet creates its own special wavy edge automatically as it is knit. Since the stitches without beads take up less space, the bracelet gets narrower as the number of beads in a row decrease.

SIZE: 8½"

MATERIALS:
14 yards strong Silver Metallic thread
12 gms Blue 10° twisted hex beads
1 pair 0000 dp steel knitting needles
Medium twisted wire needle or #10 beading needle
Hypo Cement

STRING THE BEADS:
String all twisted hex beads on a single thread.

INSTRUCTIONS:
This bracelet is knit with beads on both sides.
Cast on 10 stitches.
Row 1: Knit 10 stitches.
Rows 2-29: Follow the chart. Repeat the pattern in the chart for a total of 6 times.

Cast off, being careful to keep the cast off stitches even. Check to be certain the "cast off edge" matches the "cast on edge" in width.

Join the two edges by needle weaving together. Keep stitches even and smooth for a good join. Check each stitch from both sides.

This bracelet is especially stretchy; however, for a large hand and/or wrist, the finished size can easily be increased by repeating Rows 8 & 9 for a total of 6 rows with only 1 bead in each pattern repeat. For a small hand or wrist, eliminate Rows 8 & 9 leaving a total of 2 rows with only 1 bead.

Pattern Chart for knitted beaded wavy-edge bracelet

Rows 2 & 3	Sl st	bk st	bk st	bk st	bk st	bk st	bk st	bk st	bk st	bk st
Rows 4 & 5	Sl st	bk st	bk st	bk st	bk st	bk st	bk st	bk st	bk st	bk st
Rows 6 & 7	Sl st	bk st	bk st	bk st	bk st	bk st	bk st	bk st	bk st	bk st
Rows 8 & 9	Sl st	K st	bk st	bk st	bk st	bk st	bk st	bk st	bk st	K st
Rows 10 & 11	Sl st	K st	K st	bk st	bk st	bk st	bk st	bk st	K st	K st
Rows 12 & 13	Sl st	K st	K st	K st	bk st	bk st	bk st	K st	K st	K st
Rows 14 & 15	Sl st	K st	K st	K st	K st	bk st	K st	K st	K st	K st
Rows 16 & 17	Sl st	K st	K st	K st	K st	bk st	K st	K st	K st	K st
Rows 18 & 19	Sl st	K st	K st	K st	bk st	bk st	bk st	K st	K st	K st
Rows 20 & 21	Sl st	K st	K st	bk st	bk st	bk st	bk st	bk st	K st	K st
Rows 22 & 23	Sl st	K st	bk st	bk st	bk st	bk st	bk st	bk st	bk st	K st
Rows 24 & 25	Sl st	bk st	bk st	bk st	bk st	bk st	bk st	bk st	bk st	bk st
Rows 26 & 27	Sl st	bk st	bk st	bk st	bk st	bk st	bk st	bk st	bk st	bk st
Rows 28 & 29	Sl st	bk st	bk st	bk st	bk st	bk st	bk st	bk st	bk st	bk st

*Add a touch
of magic with the
beautiful edge on
this charming bracelet.*

Twist and Turn Lariat

by Ulla Cole

When my granddaughter saw this lariat, she immediately wanted it for a belt. This is a great accessory with multi-generational appeal. If you have daughters or granddaughters, you'd better make two, or you may not see yours very often!

SIZE: 46"

MATERIALS:
44 yards strong smooth Black polyester, silk or metallic thread
40 grams Green 8° hex beads
40 grams Crystal/Peach AB 8° hex beads
1 pair 0000 dp knitting needles
Twisted wire needle
Hypo Cement

STRING THE BEADS:
Measure: 20 yards of doubled thread and wind all but 2 yards onto a bobbin. Insert doubled thread through the eye of the needle.
String: 12 Green 8° hex • 12 Crystal/Peach AB 8° hex. Repeat 53 more times.

INSTRUCTIONS:
Cast on 4 stitches, leaving a 14" tail of thread. Knit 4 stitches.
Pattern for bead knit rows: *Slip 1 stitch • Slide 1 bead down, Knit 1 stitch • Repeat for a total of 3 bead knit stitches*.
Repeat between * and * 7 more times for a total of 8 rows knit with beads. 4 rows of knitting with beads will show on each side.
Pattern for plain knit rows: *Slip 1 stitch • Knit 3 stitches. Repeat 7 times for a total of 8 plain knit rows.

Repeat until lariat measures 36". Cast off. If there is about ½ yard of thread remaining, you will not have to add thread to make the open end tassel.

Note that the knitting gets much narrower in the plain knit rows. With a little encouragement the lariat will make a half turn between the bead knit sections, creating alternating colors on one side.

Open tassel end:
Using remaining thread from knitting, if available, you may choose to string the colors randomly or in a pattern. *String 2" of both bead colors. Bring your needle back up to the end of the lariat by threading your needle through the next to last bead in the 2" string. Bring your needle through the body of the last section knitted.* Repeat instructions between * and * for a total of 7 times. Stitch through several beads in the last knit section and finish with a knot and glue.

Looped tassel:
Using one of the long tails of thread from cast on, string 4¼" of beads, leaving approximately ½" of thread bare. Make a loop by bringing your needle back to the knitted section making sure that ½" of thread is bare on the return trip too. Repeat until there are 5 loops, switching the stringing to the other tail end after 3 loops ate complete. Stitch the shortest end of thread back into the body of the knitting and knot and glue to finish. Use the other end to wrap around the bare thread several times until the ½" of wrapping is firm. Knot and glue.

Strawberry Pin

by Deanna Van Assche

A charming ladybug bead tops this cute red strawberry pin.

SIZE: 1½" x 2½"

Tip:
When working with these small needles, work on top of your hand. Your left thumb on your work will stabilize the knitting so that you can move your beads into position.

I like to park my needle in the next knit stitch, giving me more control for moving beads.

MATERIALS:
New Metallic Threads
(#17 Ruby, #9 Emerald)
11° seed beads
(4 strands Red Silver Lined, 1 strand Green Silver Lined, 40 Black)
Lady bug bead
1 pair of 0000 knitting needles
Needles
(Wire bead, #24 Tapestry, #12 Beading)
Hypo Cement

Intermediate

STRING THE BEADS:
Transfer Red beads to the Red thread. Transfer Green beads to Green thread.

INSTRUCTIONS:
See Diagram 1. Tie a loop.
Drop thread into loop. Tighten loop. Cast on 12 stitches.

Row 1: Knit.
Rows 2-5: Knit 2, *slide 1 bead, Knit 1*, repeat 8 times, slide 1 bead, Knit 2.
Rows 6-11: Knit 2, *slide 2 beads, Knit 1, slide 1 bead, Knit 1*, repeat 4 times, slide 2 beads, Knit 2.
Rows 12-19: Knit 2, *slide 3 beads, Knit 1, slide 1 bead, Knit 1*, repeat 4 times, slide 3 beads, Knit 2.
Rows 20-25: Knit 2, *slide 4 beads, Knit 1, slide 1 bead, Knit 1*, repeat 4 times, slide 4 beads, Knit 2.
Rows 26-29: Repeat Row 12.
Rows 30-31: Repeat Row 6.
Rows 32-35: Repeat Row 2.
Rows 36-39: All Knit, no beading.
Rows 40-43: Repeat Row 2.
Rows 44-45: Repeat Row 6.
Rows 46-49: Repeat Row 12.
Rows 50-55: Repeat Row 20.
Rows 56-63: Repeat Row 12.
Rows 64-69: Repeat Row 6.
Rows 70-73: Repeat Row 2.
Change to Green thread with Green beads and continue knitting to make a leaf with 3 petals.

1. Drop thread into loop.

Hank Thread   Knitting Thread

2. Tighten loop.

3. Slide beads to knitting thread.

Tightened knot

Leaf petals:
The leaf is done in 3 sections, 4 stitches per petal, with the first 4 stitches forming petals.

Top of Leaf:
Rows 1-2: Knit 1, *slide 1 bead, Knit 1*, repeat to the end of the row.
Rows 3-4: Knit 1, *slide 2 beads, Knit 1, slide 1 bead, Knit 1*, repeat 4 times, slide 2 beads, Knit 1.
Rows 5-6: Knit 1, *slide 3 beads, Knit 1, slide 1 bead, Knit 1*, repeat 4 times, slide 3 beads, Knit 1.

First Petal:
Rows 7-8: Knit 1, slide 3 beads, Knit 1, slide 1 bead, Knit 1, slide 3 beads, Knit 1, turn work to knit back after knitting these 4 stitches. The remaining 8 stitches can stay on the needle or be placed on a stitch holder until the petal is finished.
Rows 9-10: Knit 1, slide 2 beads, Knit 1, slide 1 bead, Knit 1, slide 2 beads, Knit 1, turn work.
Rows 11-12: Knit 1, slide 1 bead, Knit 1, slide 1 bead, Knit 1, slide 1 bead, Knit 1, turn work.

Decrease as follows in the next 3 rows:
Row 13: Slip 1 stitch, Knit 1, pass Slipstitch over knit, slide 1 bead, Knit 1 bead, slide 1 bead, Knit 1.
Row 14: Slip 1 stitch, Knit 1, pass Slipstitch over knit, slide 1 bead, Knit 1.
Row 15: Knit last 2 stitches together, open loop, pass thread through loop and pull to close. Cut thread and weave thread end into petal. When weaving thread ends into each petal, use thread weaving to help shape the petal.

Second and third petals:
Reattach Green thread and repeat rows 7-15 for each petal.
Sew the ladybug bead on with one of your tails.
Sew a pin to the back of the strawberry using a piece of felt for added support.
With a tapestry needle, add the Black beads at random.
Sew the sides of the berry together.

Handle:
Anchor thread to the inside side seam. Add 2½" of beads and sew to the other side.

Amulet:
To wear the strawberry as an amulet bag, skip the pin and handle and make a 20"-26" long thread cord or beaded cord. Attach the cord to the inside seams.

*Knit a clever
little strawberry pin
in bright red.*

Small Bag

by Deanna Van Assche

This bag has the rich texture and weight of the ones I admired on my great grandmother's dressing table. Now you can knit an heirloom that your children will treasure.

SIZE: 4" x 5"

MATERIALS:
1 ball *Opera* size 20 Cotton
1 Silver frame
1 hank of 8° seed beads
1 strand bead chips
1 pair 0000 dp knitting needles
2 cards for wrapping threads
Needles (Wire beading, #24 Tapestry, #12 Beading)
Hypo Cement

STRING THE BEADS:
Thread a wire needle with cotton thread. Remove one of the threads from the hank of 8° seed beads, slide the needle under some beads to transfer to the cotton thread, then add a bead chip. Vary the number of seed beads between each chip as you continue transferring seed beads and adding a chip.

For example, 3 beads, 1 chip, 6 beads, 1 chip, 8 beads, 1 chip, 12 beads, 1 chip, 5 beads, 1 chip.

This will create an interesting texture as it is knit.

Warning: Do not load more than 6 strands of beads and not more than half of your chips. Then start knitting.

When you run out of beads, measure off the ball of yarn about 20 yards of thread and load the rest of the beads from your tail. This will help protect your thread from "over moving" the beads and you won't have any jams.

INSTRUCTIONS:

Section 1:
Cast on 32 stitches.
Rows 1-6: Knit without beads.
Rows : Knit 3, *slide 1 bead, Knit 1*, Repeat from * to * 26 times, slide 1 bead, Knit 3.
Row 8: Knit 32 stitches.
Rows 9-26: Repeat Rows 7 & 8.

Section 2:
Row 27: Cast on 2 stitches, Knit 2, *slide 1 bead, Knit 1*, repeat from * to * 28 times, slide 1 bead, Knit 2.
Row 28: Cast on 2 stitches, Knit 34.
Row 29: Knit 2, *slide 1 bead, Knit 1*, Repeat from * to * 32 times, slide 1 bead, Knit 2.
Row 30: Knit 36 stitches.
Continue repeating Rows 29 & 30 until this section measures 12".

Section 3:
Row 1: Bind off 2 stitches, Knit 3 *slide 1 bead, Knit 1*, Repeat from * to * 28 times, Knit 3.
Row 2: Bind off 2 stitches, Knit 32.
Row 3: Knit 3 *slide 1 bead, Knit 1*, Repeat 26 times, slide 1 bead, Knit 3.
Row 4: Knit 32 without beads.
Rows 5-20: Repeat Rows 3 & 4.
Rows 21-26: Knit 32 stitches without beads.

Bind off:
Sewing together: Sew bag to frame first. Center knitting, sew across, then down to increase area. Use regular sewing thread and a bead needle. Add beads to front of frame to hide sewing. After you sew both sides to frame, you are ready to sew your side seams down. Because this bag is knitted on 0000 needles and the stitches are small, it does not need to be lined.

Create this beady
little bag with colorful
beads and thread.

Pretty in Pink Poncho

by Andrea Boll

Fluffy rayon yarn makes decorative stripes in this silky poncho while randomly placed beads add texture.

When wearing the poncho the seam will run down an arm and the poncho will hang asymmetrically for a fabulous designer look.

SIZE: 14"-16" x 56"

On yarns and beads:
The poncho uses two strands held together throughout: a double strand of fingering weight cotton and a novelty yarn knit with the two strands in random stripes for added interest. Most combinations will work so be creative. Use lightweight yarn and knit looser than you typically would for a garment. This will give the poncho an airy fluid look and feel. You can knit with any gauge, just do the math so the finished measurements are the same. Beads are added randomly, or in pattern if you prefer, for added texture. Each time you add a bead just pull one up from the strand and knit it into the current stitch. If you don't use all of the beads that are strung, that is fine. They will remain on the excess yarn when the project is finished. If you run out of beads, break the yarn, add more beads and continue knitting.

MATERIALS:
300 yards double stranded yarn of a fingering weight
    and novelty yarn as desired
45 grams 6° seed beads
Size 9 and 10 straight or circular needles

GAUGE: 4¾ stitches per inch

STRING THE BEADS:
Thread the beads on the double strand of yarn, pushing them down far enough so you have plenty of yarn to work with.

INSTRUCTIONS:
Cast on 71 stitches with size 9 needles.
Row 1: Knit 3, Purl 1 ending with Knit 3.
Row 2: Purl 3, Knit 1 ending with Purl 3.
    Change to #10 needles. Repeat these 2 rows approximately 121 times or until 56" in length. Knit the last 2 rows with size 9 needles and bind off loosely leaving a long tail for sewing.

Finishing:
Fold right sides together lengthwise. We'll call the side with the long tail the top. With the long tail, sew a 16" seam on the top edge from the outside end toward the center fold. Secure well at the end as this will be one side of the neck. Tuck in ends and you're done.

Knit a pretty poncho for a fabulous designer look.

by Patricia Brink

SIZE:

10" (8½" with edge rolled up) by 20½" circumference

MATERIALS:

50 grams Yellow Worsted weight wool yarn
10 grams 6° seed beads in each color
   (Green, Purple, Red)
1 pair size 8 knitting needles or size needed
   to obtain gauge

GAUGE:

5 stitches and 7 rows to 1" in Stockinette stitch using size 8 needles

STRING THE BEADS:

String the seed beads in the color sequence indicated by the chart doing 3 repeats of each row. The first bead strung will be the last bead knit, so the stringing sequence begins at the upper left hand point. The knit (even #) rows read left to right (for stringing only) and the purl (odd #) rows read right to left. There are 3 repeats of the chart in the hat.

INSTRUCTIONS:

Knitting the Border:

Cast on 99 stitches. The hat is knit in Stockinette stitch. Starting at the lower left-hand corner, follow the chart inserting the seed beads as indicated. Row 1 is a Purl row.

The chart reads right to left for knit rows and the reverse for purl rows. To insert the seed beads, Knit or Purl a stitch, slide the seed bead up close to the stitch and Knit or Purl the next stitch. The beads will appear between the stitches on the reverse (purl) side of the fabric.

Knitting the Body:

Continue following the chart in stockinette stitch until 23 rows have been completed. For the bead pattern in the body, place the beads as indicated by knitting the beads into the stitches. The beads will appear on the right (knit) side of the fabric.

Knitting the Crown:

For the crown decreases, on row 48, Knit 9 stitches, Slip a stitch, Knit a bead into the next stitch, then pass the Slip stitch over the knit stitch with the bead, being careful to go completely over the bead. Repeat 8 more times to the end of the row. On row 50: Knit 8, Slip a stitch, Knit a bead into the next stitch, then pass the Slip stitch over the knit stitch with the bead, being careful to go completely over the bead. Repeat 8 more times. Continue in this manner decreasing every knit row until 9 stitches remain. Purl the last row.

Finishing:

Thread the yarn through the remaining 9 stitches, pull up tight and secure the yarn. Sew the side seam being careful to line up the rows. Turn up the bottom of the hat to create the rolled edge and allow the beaded rim to show.

Intermediate

Lightning Hat

Why knit the usual hat when you can add the flash of beaded lightning bolts? This hat is wonderfully soft and really fun to wear.

If you are looking for a way to brighten up the day for someone going through chemotherapy, this hat is soft enough to be a cancer cap as well.

If you choose to make this happy hat with cotton yarn, use one that has a spandex core so it will maintain its shape.

X	Green Bead - Knit in Stitch
O	Red Bead - Knit in Stitch
#	Purple Bead - Knit in Stitch
X	Green Bead - Between Stitches
O	Red Bead - Between Stitches
#	Purple Bead - Between Stitches

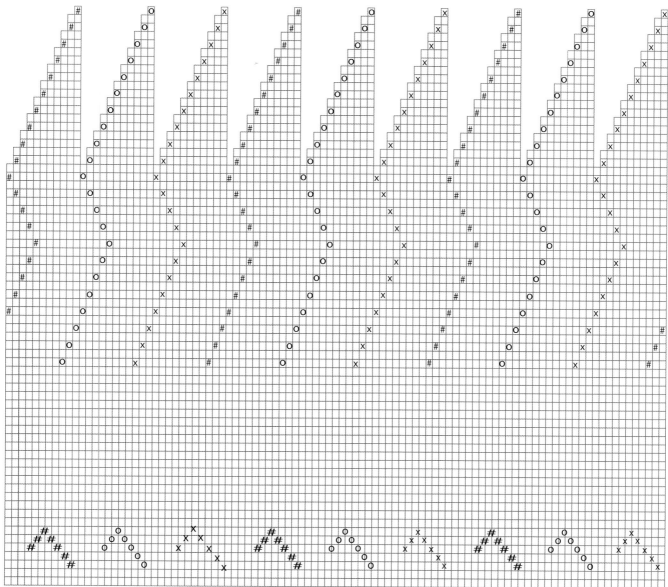

Easy

Diamond Delight Cuff
by Patricia Brink

In Norway, these cuffs are called "pulse warmers", but according to my eighth grader, these wrist cuffs and ankle bands are the hottest rage at school. Now you can make these expensive accessories in your favorite colors with exotic beads for a fun fashion statement that is uniquely and affordably yours.

SIZE:
5¼" wide x 7" circumference

MATERIALS:
50 grams (116 yards) *Falk* Dalegarn
    Periwinkle #5545 wool yarn
14 grams mixed Pastel Metallic 8° seed beads
1 pair size 5 knitting needles or size needed
    to obtain the gauge

GAUGE:
32 stitches and 32 rows to 4" or 10 cm in Knit 1 Purl 1 ribbing using size 5 needles

STRING THE BEADS:
String 165 beads.

INSTRUCTIONS:
Cast on 60 stitches. Starting at the lower right-hand corner, follow the chart. The beads are placed in the knit stitches as they are formed to create the pattern. After completing the chart, bind off and sew the two edges together to form the cuff, being careful to line up the pattern rows. Knit the second cuff to match the first.